A PRIEST OF
THE BALDY'S

A PRIEST OF THE BALDY'S

ADILEO

authorHOUSE®

AuthorHouse™
1663 Liberty Drive
Bloomington, IN 47403
www.authorhouse.com
Phone: 1-800-839-8640

Published by AuthorHouse   03/23/2012

ISBN: 978-1-4567-8476-8 (sc)
ISBN: 978-1-4567-8477-5 (e)

We all have been disappointed in our own various ways.

Jobs, friends or family, finance or love disappointments, marriage or religious disappointments, even the disappointment of not buying that child the candy you promised, we all have been disappointed one way or the other. Life in many occasions does not hand us the tools that we need in order to live, so what do we do? We get into this unending tussle and struggle to squeeze out of life the tools necessary for our survival and still it does not get any easier and that's why only the 'STRONG' survives.

Have you ever heard the story of the swinging spider? When I was 9 yrs old, my grandpa told me the story of the swinging spider. I had always wondered how these amazing eight footed bugs get from one wall to the other, amazing!

When my maximum ability cannot even my minimum objectives, goals and expectations in life… that is disappointment! I was made a man far before I became one so I inherited my World, I didn't make it… the words of a great poet and rapper of the 20th century, Lesane Crooks a.k.a Tupak Amaro Shakur.

I have learnt not to go down without a struggle… not to give up without a challenge… not to bow down and fade off without confrontation.

Since disappointment have become the way of my life, I have stared straight into the mirror through my own eyes into that dark soul and hark thou ill fated luck… for you have been weighed and found wanting!

Failure I will fight with persistence!

Bravery is the acknowledgement of fear but not submission onto it.

The sun came up a little early that day in Antwerp, the prehistoric city of Belgium. The sky as blue as it was had lots of promises for the day. Patches of the cloud hovered across the face of the heavens. The clatter of cars and trams mêlée in the air as people despatched to their various places of work. It was a kind of morning that is termed a beautiful and sunny morning.

The rays of the sun that struck the window reflected into the bedroom, caressing the face of Mr Collins. He squeezed his eyes and rolled over to the other end of the bed in a bid to evade the torture of the sun rays. Suddenly he leaped up, he had been awaken from his sleep by that radio alarm, it was as loud as a high school bell of the nineteenth century signalling the end of a midday recess. Mr Collins hastily got up and wiped his sleep away from his eyes; he reached out for the alarm and turned it out.

Mrs Collins was sleeping away in peace close to him, she was also serene an attribute by nature. She had been rather ignorant of all that noise that had ensued, her ear pads made sure of that.

I wonder how she does that, he said. He leaned over her and poked her with a finger and said;

Get up woman lets get ready to go. He is the type who would not afford to be late to an appointment when it concerns money.

She turned around slowly, with a calm voice she said

Darling, can't we stay in bed for a while. She stretched out her arms still struggling with drowsiness; it's a wonderful morning she sniggered as she struggle to open her eyelids.

A good morning it will be if you will get out of the bed we are going to be late like the other day he said huskily.

Collins had prepared endlessly for today and nothing was about to come between him and his moment. I'm trying but my stomach . . . this pain is growing strong everyday, she complained. They have been married for years but her barrenness have prevented her from the accomplishment of every woman's dream, a child.

She had been to many hospitals, many operations, many prescription but still it remained a mystery. He did not care a lot, he had other things in mind, and he's certainly not worrying for a child now.

You're what! He said on an intensed voice. I told you we should see a doctor but you won't listen. We should head for one now he said but he would rather not do that on a day he had set aside for himself. Darling, this is not a good symptom; the pain goes from my abdomen to my gullet. I hardly slept last night. She told him. That's it! Take a shower we're going to the hospital, he said cunningly. Nothing is as vital as money to him. He was not about to miss his contract rendezvous and somehow she knew that.... Oh no darling, firstly we should attend this meeting, I know how important it is to you. We'll discuss about the hospital later when we get back, she gave him a kiss and head for the bathroom.

Mr Collins hurriedly took a bath, clothed himself as presentable as possible and posed himself in the car as he waited for his wife. She finally emerge, she walked out of the door down to the car way where the car had been standing.

Mrs Collins was an appealing young woman in her late twenties, she's not what you would describe as slender by nature but her figure resemble that of a real madam. An average sized and a tolerable height with nice curvatures.

She approached the car opened the passenger's door as she came in she said, oh sorry for the delay darling, I couldn't find my necklace. She spoke always in a relaxed subtle voice.

He grimaced and said you are always looking for something.... Did u find it, as if he cared; he was rude and have forgotten how to treat a lady. No, but I'm hoping that it should be somewhere in the room ... She said but in actually it was not in the room nor was it in her necklace box and he knew that. He sold them couple of days earlier. She's not going to find out just as she couldn't find out what had happened to her expensive shoes, watches and the other stuffs which magically went missing. Maybe she does not want to know, maybe she dealt with that in an ignorant manner.

She looked at him smiled and she said . . . How do I look darling?

You look nice he said as he drove off without a glance.

But u did not even look at me, you don't care I know . . . she quietly complained.

I can't drive and look at you at the same time, we're not going to a show and I'm late for my appointment . . . he said. Yeah! Yeah, she paused for a while, viewed her face in the mirror and said as he sped down the road in high velocity. Slow down . . . we'll get there on time; there was no reply she continued . . . do you think you'll get this contract . . . Sharply he said . . . I hope so, I have to, I need it . . . I need the money . . . we need the money . . . .

Here we go again . . . she turned and gazed at him for some seconds and said

Money, money, money is all you speak about. She shook her head in dismay but he kept talking about what he would do with the money from a contract that he does not have yet, he pushed on the pedals and the car paced down the street of no great importance.

I've got a plan, with this contract, i will raise a lot of money . . . big house . . . nice car and then prepare for children, but I also can . . . she cuts in . . . Oh darling, take a look at this!

He seemed to be wrapped up in his own thought that he did not hear her. She vociferously said Look Collins . . . Look!

What! I'm concentrating, can you for one minute not interrupt me while I'm driving . . . but just then he saw it . . . it was a disturbing sight. She asked him to stop but he would not . . . . Stop the car! What was that in god's name she howled . . . he stopped, I don't know and I don't want to know.

We stopped already, they may need our help, and they don't look good . . . No, we'll just call the police and they'll handle it, I'm late for my meeting . . . . Stop being egocentric, get out of the car lets

3

see what's going on, she urged him as she opened the car door and he followed.

They walked back a few yards, and then they saw a woman on the verge panting and gasping for air, by her side was a child. She was not in a good shape neither was the little child. She was a Negro.

From her figure as she lay there, you could tell that she was a tall woman, though in despair she wore a graceful face.

They looked like they've been walking for days without food. Torn clothes and holes in both their shoes and a very gloomy look written all over their faces.

The child was about three years old considering his length and size. He did not realise the ominous situation that had befallen them he still managed a smile that melts the heart, he played alone in the middle of a lonely road next to a half dead woman.

His clothes which were bigger than him suggested that they were not his, maybe charity. The mother of the child could not speak because of lack of moisture.

Her breath did not smell good but that was obviously her least of worries. "Who are they . . . ? Where are they coming from" is something Mrs. Collins would really like to know, but for Mr. Collins, this is just another distraction to his imperative contract meeting.

Chief Okon owned the Food De Afrik shops in Antwerpen. Over the years he has managed to make a name for himself. He is now running chains of food companies all over the major cities in Belgium.

This morning he had been scheduled for a meeting to award a food importation contract to one of his solicitors. He had learned over the years not to award a contract to anyone without a face-to-face meeting. His past had thought him that. He's happily married with a three year old daughter, Arei.

His father came from the kingdom of the Nzere people, currently called the Republic of Zaire. His ancestors had paid the immense price of death during the olden time of King Leopold 1 of Belgium and the Zairean rubber business.

A whole lot of Zaireans live in Belgium the land of their colonial masters who had dealt a great blow of injustice to their forefathers in the past. Just as a crucifix signifies the redemption image of a Christian so did a German sheppard an agonising image of the ancient Zairean people.

Those dogs where used to hunt them down, while many would loose parts of their body if they refused co-operation in the then on-going rubber business. But that was in the past and life must go on.

Chief Okon, as he was called, chieftaincy entitled by his fortune.He was in a scurry to get to the office. He hurried to the car but was surprised at what he saw . . . . hello my angel, what a surprise! . . . How are we doing today? Though he was astounded to find little Arei all dressed up and waiting in the car. He did not remember making such arrangement but he tried not to show his astonishment.

Good morning papa. Arei said. she was adorable. The only child of a rich man, of course she got often her request . . . . What are you doing in the car this morning? He asked.

I'm going to the office with you. She replied . . . Sorry dear, it'll be a very busy day for me so stay home and help mama. It's boring at home and its holidays. She frowned and crinkled her arms. Mama spends a lot of time on the phone, she added.

I guess that's a no . . . he heaved a sigh. He acted as if he needed sometime to think about it then he said, Ok! But promise to be quiet while I handle my interview . . . he asked her with a broad paternal grin. Arei smiled and nodded a yes to her father who smiled back and gave her a kiss.

I love you papa Arei said . . . . I love you my angel, and what is the first rules when we get into the car, he asked . . . fasten your seat belt! She yelled back while she sent out a tiny cute glee. She was glad that finally she would not have to sit at home and watch her mother on the phone with the women of her country club tittle-tattle the whole day away.

That's right my angel and here we go . . . as he pulled out of the drive way onto the streets.

Chief had gone for a while when it struck him that he should tell Mrs. Okon that Arei was with him.

While driving he picked up his phone and dialled his wife. The phone rang for a few seconds and there came a voice from the other end . . .

Hello, I got in the car this morning and had a little surprise . . . but before he started talking she fretfully said . . . Is Arei with you?

Yes dear, I was just telling you of a surprise . . . Oh thank God! I could not find her anywhere; I was worried she exhaled . . . I should have told you before we left but don't worry I'm going to have my secretary take care of her, he assured her.

I couldn't find her in her room; I just was about ringing you. She kept on reciting.

Sorry, I should have told you, I won't be long at the office so we'll be seeing you . . . he didn't finish those words when Chief heard her little girl scream . . . Papaaaaaaaaa!

His reaction was couple of seconds late.

There have been a deardful car crash and the line went dead. Mrs Okon heard vividly the noise of rumbling metals; she immediately knew something dreadful had happened.

Hello! Hello! Dear! Arei! Hello! She kept screaming and lamenting

Oh my God! This can't be! Oh my God! She snivelled a bit and ran into the bedroom grabbed her bag and ran off.

Mrs Collins was the first to get to the woman and the child who lay by the roadside.

Oh my God! Collins gets over here, take a look at this . . . she gestured towards them but he was not as sympathetic as she had been.

Mr Collins looked over his left and right shoulders and grudgingly walked over to her . . .

He said . . . Oh no! No! No! No! I knew I should not have listened to you . . . a Black man in the middle of no where with a dying woman and a kid . . . what will I tell the police . . . When the get here . . . . listen carefully woman, get in the car right now and I am not asking you . . .

It's a child! Damn it! Mrs Collins said and before she could finish, he cuts in and said

Woman, you've been sent to demolish me, to destroy my life so people back home will chuckle at me. Stories of how I killed people for money would be all over the town, abi? Get out from there. Let the police handle that. She got up and was about to leave when the dying woman moved her head and said Something . . .

Please help my child, don't go please . . . she was as weak as fish on a dry land.

She came closer but could still not hear her so she bent over her and said

What did you say . . . ? What happened to you . . . who are you . . . questions plunged out of her

Mount like water . . . the woman took a deep breath tried to gather enough strength that would

Enable her speak louder . . .

I beg you lady. Don't leave my child here. Please help him . . .

Who are you . . . ? And what's your name . . . the questions kept coming. None of her questions had been answered but she didn't stop asking . . . finally she said

It's not important. Important is my child . . . Please help me! What's your son's name? she asked . . .

He is Raphael! He's a good kid and he's all I have. She painted heavily and coughed up some slimy fluid . . . She had already dialled the ambulance.

Hang on, don't give up, the ambulance is on the way. You'll be taken to the hospital and you will be fine."

She smiled with pains and whispered something that sounded like a relief then she turned at Mrs Collins and she said . . ."Promise me that you won't leave my child . . . Promise me please!

It's ok. Your child will be fine. I will be here till you are safe. Mrs Collins said convincingly.

Yes I know . . . The woman said; assure me that you will take care of my child.

She looked around, looked up to the sky as if God was watching her to know what sort of choice she'ld make in a time like that and then she said . . . Ok, I promise". She would promise anything to keep her alive.

Thank you and I know you will . . . Just as she said that, she gasped and exhaled her last breath with the child in the arms Mrs. Collins.

No, no! Don't die! she screamed crying and quivering . . . Just then Mr. Collins came to his right mind and ran towards Mrs. Collins and the lifeless woman and said . . .

Is she dead? She can not die! What! Oh no, he was terrified . . . We have to go now . . . he said impulsively. He hauled her away from the corpse leaving the child in the bosom of a dead mother. You have to leave the child here and get out now . . . he screeched

Let the police will take care of him . . . He kept telling her as he dragged her towards their car.

He sat her in the passenger's seat and shot the door. Then he walked fast crossing over to the drivers seat in a move for a nippy getaway . . . he kept emitting profanities at her that he did not even notice what had happened.

She had jumped out of the car before he could get to the drivers seat. She wouldn't stop pronouncing to herself . . . I promised! I promised! As she ran towards the abandoned child and the dead poor stranger.

As she ran to them, she could hear the ambulance approaching and what sounded like a police car. She slowly took the child took a good gawk at the dead woman as if she could run into her someday and then she sorrowfully said . . . I gave you my word and I won't lie to the dead.

She took the child made back to the car. Mr Collins still angry and cursing didn't

Notice her leave the car. He was about driving away when he saw her via the rear mirror running towards the car with the boy, he stopped and said . . . This can't be true! This is not happening!

He placed his hands his head in great aggravation just as she got in the car with the child and sat him down on her lap.

Now, we can go! She said. You can't be serious . . . there's no way I'm driving away with an unknown child in my car . . . he answered. If they had seen an unknown amount of money on the street, it would not have mattered to him. He would not hesitate to have kept it. He just had his priorities and saving a child is not one of them. No time to argue lets go please! She begged but he was adamant.

There's no time to debate, as the sirens got closer the noise grew louder for little Raphael. He held tight to her as he sped off, the kid watched the remains of his mother disappear into the narrow street.

While driving away from the scene, Collins was furiously upset with his wife.

Woman what have you done! Everybody knows we have no child! What is wrong with you! I'm not going down like this . . . he raged.

She was still in a state of huge uncertainty, shaking as she held tight to the child. Not knowing if she acted right or wrong she kept saying to herself . . . I promised! I promised.

Who . . . what are you talking about . . . he asked. He did not really seek an answer to that question but she replied. I promised her to look after her child. I did not think that she was going to die. I just promised.

Don't tell it to me! Tell it to the police . . . . I don't want to hear anything! He said.

I could not leave the child there . . . I don't intend to now. She replied.

Maybe for the first time, he actually felt that she was not about to leave the child.

He tried being reasonable and said to her . . .

You don't know that woman or this child! What if he's not her child . . . ? Have you thought of that! I know u want a child but this is an abduction and we can go to jail, no . . . no not we! You can go to jail for a long time woman! I won't visit you in jail and won't go with you either. Give the child up now! Collins lectured on.

The child looked up at her as if he understood the words of her husband.

Don't be scared Raphael, you are safe with me she assured him and tears fell down her cheek.

She took his hands and wrapped them around her to confirm her promise to him, something eccentric took place, she instantaneously felt a swift flash of heat through the boy's hands exceed via her ribs down to her lower haunch and up into her womb. At once the boy was covered with sweat and he passed out.

This all happened very fast, she could not understand what it was and surely not in that circumstance and since it did not last for long she thought it was her imagination. When she noticed that the boy had passed out she yelled at him to stop the car. Stop the car! Something is wrong with the child.

Precisely my point! He said scornfully as he turned and saw the boy motionless on her lap.

What a day! My meeting! My dreams everything is falling apart . . . did I not warn you,

He blamed her. She checked his pulse; the child's pulsation was weak. She became totally confused and afraid.

His pulsate was very slow. We need to get him to the hospital now. She told him.

That I will not do! We have no documents to identify him, we can not go the hospital, we can leave him here and the police will find him, this is your last opportunity he growled

Out of irritation and utter despair she said . . . if this child dies, you don't want to know what I am competent of telling the police.

He saw the rage in her eyes; it was nothing like he had ever seen in her. This was the other side of this decent woman he had married many years ago.

So now you are threatening me! He said cautiously . . . .

Move the car to the hospital she bawled as he pedalled off to Saint Jens Hospital in Stuivenberg, the nearby hospital which was about ten kilometres away.

At Stuivenberg, which is known as one of the best hospitals in Western Europe. The doctors could not diagnose his ailment. His trempreture measured well, he had no sign of fever or cold. He was kept and monitored for security reasons in accordance to the doctor's pre-scribtion. After several days he got better and went on to live with the Collins family.

Mrs Collins inexplicably got pregnant twice and had a boy and a girl, Michael and Nikki.

Raphael grew up with this unexplained clout of healing. During his elementary school days, he healed many people young and old till his step-father came up with his repugnant plot of exploitation.

He had a knotty time growing up, he was particular and gifted but he had a very unique look which was not assimilated by the other kids . . . He had no tresses.

His was so bald that you could use them for a mirrow. He was called names and taunted by other kids but he was the saving grace of Mrs Collins and she loved him like her own.

Why do the other kids hate me, Raphael would ask his mother . . . They do not hate you my son. You are very special and they do not understand you because they are afraid. You are just different in a way they don't know and people tend not to accept things they don't know. I know you and you are my son she would conclude as she watched him smile.

He got along very fine with his siblings.

Many years have passed and Raphael grew into a handsome lad. He had two younger ones . . . named Michael and Nikki. His siblings did not know how they came to be.

Mrs Collins was not certain of that, so she mentioned it to nobody.

The life of Raphael as a youth is not what you would call an easy or a smooth one. His mysterious power had condemned his chances of having a normal life.

Even when he does not choose to be noticed, his ability works for itself. He could not control his gift from above whenever he comes in contact with a sick or wounded person.

The families that he had cured their loved ones would shower him with gifts but he never took any.

His baldness had earned him a special look, one that often scared little children.

When he was in the fourth grade, two kids in his class where fighting over the ownership of a pen when suddenly the situation escalated and spilled more blood in the classroom than that of a high speed car crash. His class kids all ran into the hall way screaming as they trampled over one another in that intensed getaway bid.

Their teacher had received a call from the head Mistress earlier. The class was vacated in a matter of minutes, those who had guts hanged by the classroom window while they watched the poor little Hans bleed his life away.

In the classroom, one little boy was left, fearless and brave he stood. He became the last boy standing. He was Raphael. He knelt beside the draining little Hans not knowing why . . . he did not run like the other kids did though he wanted to. Hans looked up and saw Raphael, he put forth his right hand while he held his bleeding eye with the left hand and in shock he said . . . Raphael, please don't go, please I'm afraid, he kept asking him not to leave. He was so steady and still, he did not move as he kept nodding a yes to the boy. When the boy's hands finally touched Raphael's wrist, he grabbed him and did not want to let him go. Just then their teacher who had been notified of the tragic accident ran into the classroom and what he saw was something that changed the history of St. Patricks Memorial Primary school.

Raphael in full swing quivered like he had been struck by lightening, the tremble was so great that it caused a mini whirl wind and a huge amount of what seemed like a white flash missed in cloudy smoke over shadowed the two boys.

When the smoke, the wind, the cloud and the light disappeared, the boy who had been stabbed with blood all over his face had been totally healed and well. The smoke and the light had licked away all the blood and his eye was restored. It was very swift. He knelt over Raphael who lay motionless on the floor. The class kids who watched from the window took to their heels. Mr Van Kirk, the class teacher fled.

After several days in the hospital, Raphael was discharged from the hospital.

He became a hero and a freak. The parents of little Hans offered him gifts but he would not accept. After that incident, it became obvious to his mother what had happened seven years ago.

This was indeed the beginning of his healings. The doctor had told his mother that though Raphael is a unique kid and quite normal but that there was something about his brains that troubled him. He advised her to keep him away from stress till he could find a clue to what he had seen under the scan. This happened a decade ago.

Ten years later, his 20th birthday, his brother's 17th and his sister's 14th.

His family had grown into a semi-mature family. His loving mother and money-freak father all lived under the same roof.

Raphael did not stop healing and making others happy, his step father had gone away from Mrs Collins because she would not give in to his idea of dumping a helpless child, he had returned when he heard that she was of child. In many occasions, he would arrange for many sick people and as long as he got paid, he did not complain. Raphael and the rest of the family knew nothing of his treachery.

Michael and Nikki were two captains on the same boat and you know what they say about that.

They argued quite a lot . . . as much as they got along they fought as well.

One afternoon, they agreed on playing a game to relax. On a weekend, they had not gone to school. They had only played for a quarter of an hour when someone rang the door bell.

Are you expecting someone Nikki asked . . . no, but get the door, Michael replied.

You get the door! If I move you'll cheat! She complained.

I won't, I promise. He said . . . Ok stop, I'm watching you!

As she back peddled to the door . . . took the intercom handle and said,

Yeah! Who's there . . . ?

She listened into the earpiece of the intercom and then looked at him . . . she scowled and said . . . Michael, it's your white ass Barbie doll gal friend

Stop calling her names and hurry up and open the door . . . he said excitedly. Don't yell at me, I'm opening . . . Nikki murmured.

She pressed the lock and let the visitor in. Then she went and sat beside him with folded hands and said . . . here goes our day, what do you see in her . . . you betrayer of your race.

Michael looked at her and hissed just then the door opened and a white girl came in with a smile . . . She was very well dressed . . . a typical Hispanic European, the type Michael would always go for and Nikki had always disliked.

Hey guys . . . the visitor said. She made herself quite comfortable. She is no guest after all.

Hey Sandy . . . Nikki replied in a voice that almost sounded repulsive.

Michael Looked at his sister as to say stop that sarcastic behaviour.

Hi babe! how are you doing? Michael asked her.

He walked to her and kissed her passionately for a while . . . and while they're busy kissing and smooching, Nikki growled and said. Get a room Michael or better still get your own house. She hated her for always stealing her brother away when she mostly needed him.

What's wrong with her? Sandy asked . . . .

Just ignore her, she ran out of luck today . . . The car race game was no fun for her . . . he answered.

Oh! I see! . . . . She turned to Nikki and mockingly she said, Too bad Nikki, as she winked at her . . . . Speaking of the game guys, do you have space for one more, Sandy continued.

Sure baby . . . don't we Nikki? Michael said as he turned to Nikki.

I'm done anyway, both of you can knock yourselves out . . . I'm going to check on my brother. Nikki quickly replied chillingly.

Mama told you to leave Raphael alone, remember? He reminded her.

Who says I'm bugging him, mind your own business . . .

She pointed at the white fine stature as she left the scene.

Girls! Girls. He said as he turned to his visitor.

And I heard that, unfortunately I'm one of them. Sandy mocked

No baby, not you . . . You're so cool and different . . . He told her as they kissed and walked to his room.

Raphael sat in his room reading a fresh version of a James Hardly Chase's Novel, he liked the romance genre. The miracle boy who had been picked up by the roadside and though Mrs. Collins never told him nor Nikki and Michael had no clue of his past.

Those three knew themselves as family and she loved him well.

His greedy father who left their mother because she refused to give up Raphael came back after he learnt that Mrs. Collins was of child but he still remained a money conscious son-of-a-bitch.

Raphael has the power to heal and so he is special and different from other kids. They other kids saw him as a freak, at school they called him names like: nigger vampire, voodoo king, black wizard, priest of the baldies.

Raphael being different in colour and strength have learned to be on his own. Only at home with his siblings he felt free and normal.

His greedy father had turned his divine ability to a money making avenue for his private portfolio.

Raphael isolated himself and built a wall between himself and the outside world, but his powers were needed and have made many families happy.

Raphael is a fine looking young man but he had few weird looks. He was bald from childhood, no hairs have grown on his head and face but he was quite hairy on his chest.

He had always kept to himself and could hardly make friends.

His father made himself rich by demanding money from the families of the many he had cured without his son's knowledge. He used the divine powers of Raphael to meet his financial demands and still pretended to be poor.

Mrs Collins paid all the bills while he drowned himself in liquor and women. Mrs Collins was a naïve woman, she was also raised the sole traditional way.

When Mr Collins discovered that Raphael is a child with a special gift, he tried convincing his wife of the profit they would make by using him as a medium but she bluntly turned him down. He then would go behind them and collect money from the families of the sick who had been cured or yet to be cured. He would tell them that Raphael had demanded for that wage. He made a lucrative sum of money at the expense of poor Raphael.

Mrs. Collins did not really keep a good married relationship with Mr. Collins. She had given divorce many thoughts but because of her Christian beliefs she couldn't bring herself to file for one, even she knows that the platform of marriage which is trust and happiness has been absent for a long while. What kept them together was as thin as a black thread. The kids are her major concern and concentration.

Raphael particularly had been a child of promise and she was not about to give up her promise to the dead. His well being was her priority

While Raphael read his novel, a tiny knock on his door interrupted his concentration. He stopped and listened to make sure he heard something but the silence continued and so he turned back to his book. He had actually heard a knock but was not sure of what he heard. Another tiny scratchy knock came, this time he knew exactly what he heard and who it could be.

Go away Nikki, I'm busy! But she kept going on with that annoying twitchy knock.

Finally, a voice came from behind the door. hey Raphy can I come in?

No Nikki . . . I'm reading . . . he replied

I need to tell you something . . . she said

Say it, I can hear you from over there. He answered

Come on Raphy! Please! Please . . . she kept persuading him

Just before she said her unending please, the door opened just wide enough for Raphael to put his head out,

What is it Nikki? Why are you bothering me? He said still holding his guard

Can I come in as she pushed her way through.

Raphael followed behind and said . . . . Can I stop you, What is it . . . ?

I just want to see how you are doing . . . . Nikki said

Thank you my good sister . . . did Michael send you out of the living room? He asked

Nikki nodded with a look on her face that defined how innocent she had been and how Michael had discarded her from the living room.

Do not give me that look, you must have done something, if you want to stay here, promise not to disturb me or I'm going to tell mum. He demanded

Nikki Sharply said . . . I wont i promise.

Across your heart? He motioned her to do so . . . as she drew a cross sign on her chest.

Raphael laughed, drew her close to him and gave her a kiss on her forehead, hugged her and took a deep breath.

Nikki sat in a corner. she stared at Raphael every now and then as if she had to get something off her chest but since she promised not to disturb him she could only but stare. He got tired of her stare and said in a calm voice . . . ok Nikki, you can tell me what is troubling you.

Raphy . . . as she fondly called him

Yes. he answered quietly

How does it feel to be like you. she had asked, I mean I know how it feels to be your sister, how I'm regarded on the street . . . Some of my friends don't want to talk about you when they see me, they would prefer to speak in my back. I know I shouldn't feel bad but sometimes I do. I wish they could see what a great person you are and the great things you do . . . Sometimes, I do wish you were like every other guy.

Raphael took a deep breath and said . . . Sometimes I wish like you do little sister, I'm sorry for all what you and this family go through. I am your brother and it doesn't matter what people say, I'll always be your brother. I am not like every other guy, I am who I am. and I love you, he assured her. Nikki came to him, she hugged him and held him firm.

He had a infinite brotherly emotions for her. His super natural power was given to him, it was not his choice to be who he is. He knew that his family was his place of sanity and he loved them with a pure heart.

If they bug you again I'll change all of them into a stone, he joked . . . Nikki quickly gazed at him as if that would be an option, he winked at her and they both laughed.

Mrs. Collins prepared cereal, some nicely scrambled eggs and toasted bread, orange punch and pineapple syrup and Nikki was her aid in the kitchen and the dinner table was made for a family breakfast, a routine Mrs Collins had kept for a long time.It had always been her way of getting familiar with the kids daily program and she really cherished the moment.

Mr Collins sat down and waited for what seems to be the favourite meal of the day. He had in his hands the morning journal. He sat himself down to devour as much as he could of the deliciously prepared meal. His selfishness would not let him wait for the rest of the family. Just when breakfast was being served, Nikki yelled.

Raphy and Michael! Breakfast is ready!

Nikki, you can simply go to their rooms and wake them up . . . her mother said

I'm going to get Raphy . . . so she choose to do. Apparently the game of yesterday and the white girl still lingered on her mind

On Raphy's way down to breakfast Mrs. Collins told him to go and get his brother so they would all eat together.

Mr. Collins who paid little or no attention to his household, busy with his papers said. Kids of these day lacks discipline, back in Africa when I was a kid, i would go to the stream three miles away before breakfast. He had no discipline and certainly no humanity.

Not now darling . . . she said, let us enjoy this morning meal in peace. He argued always and would take no correction.

Not now! . . . ? When . . . ? Spoilt kids running around the house, you should go to Africa and see what upbringing is all about, you're telling me not now . . . he scolded.

This is not a good table manner darling . . . she tried to calm him down

Oh! . . . Table manners right! Here you have tables, in Africa we eat on the floor, so how the hell should I have your so called table manners huh . . . ? and where is that Michael! He screamed.

Raphael went to Michael's room and knocked. Knock! Knock!

Michael come on breakfast is ready and we are all waiting for you. Raphael said.

Michael's bedroom door was slightly open and he could hear him snore heavily.

He was a heavy sleeper, one that could sleep even under a heavy rainfall and would not be bothered. They called him the zombie. He pushed the door open and saw a naked white girl sleeping next to Michael. It was the first time he had ever seen a naked woman. He gazed at her for a second in shock and nervousness then turned his face away. He quickly stepped back to the door and looked away from her. He yelled out to Michael. In trembling lips.

The sleepy boy answered . . . Yeah, I'll be right there!

He Stormed out of that place like a rocket to the dinningroom to inform his mother that Michael was on his way. He avoided eye contact with anyone as he spoke.

Are you ok? His mother asked

Yeah, I'm fine . . . eh mum, can I eat up in my room? Raphael said

Sure you can! Nikki will bring you something to eat if you want. She replied. She knew something had happened but did not want to push any further.

Nikki said . . . Yeah Raphy, I'll get it for you, as if she understood what just went down

Thanks . . . he said as he hurried up to his room.

He had never given it a thought, though he read a lot of romantic books he never thought it was something for him. When he saw his own younger brother with a woman, he again remembered how different he had been and it troubled him.

He wondered why something that would have made him famous was breaking down his life.

If he could stripe himself of this power, maybe he would grow hairs, may be he could have a girlfriend or even experience love. All this may-be are probably not made for one as uniquely cursed as he is. Could there be hope for him, could it be that there is a God indeed, Raphael is yet to find out.

On a Sunday afternoon while he sat in his room as he often did. He had just past the tenth page of his novel when he had a knock on his door. He knew that it was not the sluggish knock of his kid sister, besides Sunday had been a day Nikki would not sit home. She explored the city of Antwerp every Sunday in company of friends.

Mr. Collins Knocked twice on his door. Yeah, who's there? Came a sharp reply from the inside . . . Mr Collins answered, Hello Raphael, it's me. Dad? He asked. He knew something was up. Mr

Collins was not a habitual visitor of his son. He got up and opened the door . . . Come in, he said.

Mr. Collins strolled in with his hands in each pocked of his trousers.

How are you today? He asked him . . .

It made him anxious and even more suspicious of his visit. Cordial speeches were not Mr Collins strong qualities, indeed he had none.

I'm fine dad. he replied waiting for his actual reason to surface.

We have not spoken for a while son, so I thought we catch up a bit . . . he shrug so he went on, is there something you need.? Mr Collins asked

Raphael answered quickly . . . No dad, I'm fine, thanks.

Mr. Collins persuaded him . . . Nothing at all? Are you sure?

Raphael took a good look at his father and said.

Tell me dad, what do you want?

He brought out his right hand out of his pocket and rubbed his chin and stroked his head as if he was hesitating, then he brought out the other hand and started his story.

Listen son, I know that I promised you that the last time was going to be the last, but listen . . .

But listen to what dad? We had a decision and you promised me after what I went through that it was the last . . . Raphael said sharply. He had done that earlier and Raphael had been hospitalized after his encounter with a man who was dying of diabetes. He had been severely ill . . . Yes I know, hear me out . . . The daughter of my boss . . .

Just as he mentioned "the daughter" the naked white girl's image who he had seen days back on Michael's bed came into his mind. He visualized it again and hissed. Meeting girls are certainly not the top on his list.

No dad, no way . . . you promised and you have to stick by it. He said.

I want to, I swear but I'll loose my job because I already promised my boss that my son will help his daughter. Hospitals and many doctors could not help her. She's so young Raphael, please help her! He begged

No I wont! I'm not God . . . Leave me alone and get out of my room! Raphael insisted. For the first time, Raphael stood up for himself. He was tired of all the names he had been called, how he'd been used and how he probably won't have a girl added up to his frustration, he got tensed and he screamed at his father and cried, the noise got the attention of the others and in came rushing the whole family. He shivered and sweated heavily in the arms of his mother and suddenly he fell into a trance.

In his trance, he dreamt of a girl in pain and sore affliction. She was so beautiful and charismatic, he instantly fell in love with her. At first her face was glittering like the stars, it looked as if she was transfiguring in to a fine little fairy. The kind of you see in cindrella adventure movies.

She looked at him and said help me, but he didn't understand her. What kind of help would someone almost as perfect as she is needed but suddenly Raphael saw himself in a different version of his trance and this time the same girl really needed help, a whole lot of it. She was transformed into a very sick person, not looking flourishing, rather she looked ill and she was in great misery as if she was about giving up the ghost. But one thing connected her resemblance from the first dream, her smile.

She didn't stop smiling at him as she gently reached out for him and with a transparently smile she said: Help me! Raphael!

Raphael was confused, he didn't know what to do, he reached out to take her hands but he couldn't. He tried to understand why she could be so sick and yet share such a beautiful smile.

Who are you? He asked, still reaching out for her hands. She kept smiling didn't answer the question but kept saying, help me; as she evaporated into thin bubbles of moiste air. She was taken away from him and all he heard was the re-echoing of her voice fading away into the dark seeking for his help . . . Please help me! Help me! Help me!

Raphael called out for her, Wait! . . . Please don't go please! Who are you? Where are you going? Who are you? He repeatedly asked as he struggled on his bed.

He woke up frightened. He panted and sweated heavily as he realized he had been dreaming. He looked around and saw his mother sitting next to his bed. She had been there for a while.

When Raphael got up, Mrs. Collins was sleeping on the chair next to Raphael's bed. She got up with a worried look and went to her son, she held his hand and said . . .

Son, it's just a dream son, it's ok! Mama is here!. Mr Collins had long been gone.

Raphael looked at her with tired eyes and asked her how long he'd been in that trance. He would sometimes go into trance for days when he got stressed. The doctor had warned his mother to keep him out of such stress and she's making sure of that to the extent that she could.

How long have I been out this time mother . . . he asked

Mrs. Collins tried to force a smile . . . It's not important son, you're back now and that's all that mattered, she replied. Each time he would go into a trance, she had always feared that he might not come back and each time he recovered, she would be greatly relieved. So it does not matter how long as long as he came back.

I had a dream mom. He said with an un-usual face.

What was it about? She waited impatiently.

I don't know how to say this. it's quite scary he went on . . . he looked at her and said it's about a woman.

She was surprised. Raphael knew nothing about women. Mrs Collins was sure of that.

I want to hear about it son! Please tell me. she said

First I saw her shinning like a star, smiling at me. She looked at me like she knew everything about me. Then said: help me, still smiling. he narrated

And do you know her? She asked in panic. Many things crossed her mind. She never told him about his real mother, she did not have to bring him into the past especially when it's not an inspiring one. He had enough miseries in his life so why add more she had always argued with herself. Raphael is a gifted child so she could not rule out the possibility of him having dreams that could reveal where he had come from. Could this woman be his biological mother trying to reach her son from the land beyond. How disappointed he would be if he found out. Her mind kept racing till he said . . .

Mother, I'm home all the time. Where and how could I have met a woman . . . ? I don't know her, never seen her before! Raphael said.

She adjusted her seat comfortably and softly said.

I'm sorry son, that was a wrong question. so he continued

I didn't think she was serious because she kept smiling but suddenly I found my self in this horrible place and same girl was laying there looking really sick, I could recognize her because she kept smiling at me just the way she did at first as she cried out to me for help in pains. Suddenly she vanished but I could still hear her plea.

When she heard of the girl's disappearance, she shrugged and said . . . . Let her go my son . . . let her go!

No mom, you don't understand. He said

Son, I understand that she's a ghost! She said

I doubt it mom. Raphael insisted.

Then his door opened and Michael and Nikki came in.

Hey man, are you ok? Michael asked

He nodded with a gentle smile.

Michael told him he had all of them worried.

Just then Nikki sprang on his bed and laid beside him.

She was the kid of the of the house. She promised him that she won't go out on Sundays anymore but he told her not to worry that everything was well.

Still I won't go out anymore . . . she said

Raphael Smiled at her and nodded an ok.

She hugged him and they sat in his room and conversed on.

At the office Mr Collins sat on his desk with his phone on his ears and gazed at the window probably planning one of his mischievous moves when he had a knock. Hold on he said to the person on the phone . . . he looked towards the door and said, Come in.

The door opened and an elderly gentleman came in accompanied by two others who looked more like bodyguards. He quickly put back the phone to his mouth and said . . . .I'll call you back.

Hello Chief, how are you . . . he addressed the gentleman.

I wish I could say the same after you have been avoiding me, Mr. Collins. Chief Okon said

I didn't remember that we had an appointment today, he said rather astonished.

Chief Okon said . . . Well, that's because we didn't have any today.

Mr. Collins went on. Oh I see, because I wouldn't forget an appointment with you.

He was getting comfortable at his flattery when Chief Okon caught in and said . . .

We had one but it was two weeks ago . . . with a grumbling and angry voice he continued

You see Mr. Collins, I'm a very busy man and I don't have time to waste, especially not when my daughter's life depended on it.

Mr. Collins said . . . Chief, please let me explain.

No Mr. Collins, let me rather explain this to you!

If these was not an issue of my daughter's life being in the hands of your so-called mystery son, I swear on my mother's grave and may her soul rest in peace . . . he did the sign of the cross and kissed his fingers and continued his speech . . .

You would be sleeping with the fishes by now. But I'll give you one more week to make me happy or bring back my money! Do you understand that?

Mr. Collins in terrible panic said . . . Yes, yes, of course!

He jiggled in accordance to his answer.

Good, very good! . . . Chief stared straight into his eyes some mini seconds to make sure he got the message and stormed out of the office with his bodyguards.

Mr. Collins went back to his seat breathing heavily. He thought of what to do, how to solve the situation because Chief Okon is highly respected and rich and he had already been partially paid.

While he was engulfed in this delicate situation, his phone rang.

He took it and made sure it wasn't chief Okon, then he listened and when the voice was vividly different from that of Chief's voice he screamed . . . Not now . . . .! I said not now damn it!

He turned out his phone and threw it on the table and he went back to what seemed to be his vital problem which at the moment was Chief Okon.

If only that boy would listen . . . if only i could convince him.

But how? He would not even take anything from me.

Over shadowed in his thought, he realised that finally his game was coming to an end.

If Chief Okon would descend on him, hell would have no fury. He knew he had to act fast.

Mr. Collins drove from his office to see Raphael. Mr. Collins has not seen Raphael since the incident at home but has decided to visit him for his own safety. It has always been like that, he had always been a selfish fellow and a bad father. Now that he's in a fix he would do whatever to crawl out.

Raphael sat in front of the television on a sofa. watching the national geography programme. He loved watching the animals together in their habitat. Something he called a perfect world. He would sometimes fear that if men would go to heaven, they may change the laws and serenity of that place. In no time, heaven could become a chaotic place of war and hatred. He thought that human beings given enough time can wreck heaven so he concluded that heaven is only fit for animals. Because of what his unknown powers had brought him, Raphael feared things of the unknown world.

While he enjoyed his program, the sound of the openning door called his attention back. First he hesitated and then reduced the sound of the television but the door opened and Mr. Collins came in.

Mr. Collins said . . . Hello son.

Rubbing his both hands as if he had been out in the snow. He stepped into the room.

Hey dad . . . how was it today, he asked with a with a smile.

Mr. Collins answered . . . Not very bad, how are you doing? as he sat himself down on the sofa.

Raphael replied . . . Better, I feel better.

Mr. Collins started with his speech as if he cared . . . It's been really hard for the family,especially you it's been really tough . . . he sweet talked.

For one to see his own child in this situation is really difficult, people keep expecting things from you and yet they give back nothing. he kept going. If only Raphael knew how rich his step father had become and all his deeds their conversation won't hold.

Yeah dad, I know how difficult it's been for all of you.

I'm really sorry! I wish I could do something to help it, I'm sorry dad. Raphael said. His emotion came over him. But his father was unto something else, a green snake in a green yard.

Mr. Collins took something as if he was considering his condolence and continued . . . It's ok son, it's not your fault, just the way things are . . . your dad is really having it difficult but I shouldn't complain because you're having it even more difficult than we're son. If you need me I'll be there for you ok!

He got up and gave him a Judas kiss on his forehead. He played the nice guy to his best.

I'll let you rest now ok son, hope you get better soon! I love you son, I know I should say it often but I do.

He made towards the stairs hoping that he would be stopped. then Raphael said

Hey dad! Mr. Collins turned around excitedly and said . . . Yeah son! He answered

Em . . . . That girl . . . . Raphael said but didn't finish as Mr Colins answered . . . What girl?

The sick girl. He continued

Mr. Collins pretentiously said . . . . Oh! Yeah that girl . . . don't worry about her, her faith is in God's hands!

She is still sick? He asked

Yeah, she is still sick. He said as he shrugged.

I want to see her. Can you arrange that? He asked

Mr. Collins reluctantly said . . . I don't know, maybe.

Try to do that dad! Ok! Raphael persuaded him

Yeah, sure! He smiled and left the room.

Mr. Collins went up to his room and flipped open his cell phone and dialled some numbers.

Hello Chief . . . he talked into the mouth piece.

Chief sat in his car when his phone rang. Yeah, who is this?

This is Mr. Collins on the line. Came the answer.

Chief asked if he could be of any help to him.

Oh no! no! Just to know when you are ready to bring your daughter. My son is ready to receive her.

Chief Okon was very pleased. He replied in a cool manner being careful not to show him how excited he felt . . . Well, Mr. Collins, that's good news, very good for your sake! I'll make some calls and we'll talk later.

That's good. You see Chief, I was wondering if you can bring me the rest of the money, I'm really in a huge financial fix and I'll be really . . . Hello! Hello

Chief Okon are you there?"

He hung up and looked around as if he had been fooled, then he shook his head.

Chief Okon had hung up as he mentioned money.

Mr Collins had weeks earlier received from Chief a huge amount of money as he promised him that his son would make Chief's daughter whole again.

Raphael was a bit nervous about the sick girl who was coming to get healed. This was not the first time that he had recieved this kind of challenge. He tried to find answers to his recent state of mind as he laid on his bed and spoke to himself.

Why am I so nervous? I've done this before. What's the difference now? He asked himself.

He got up from the bed went to the window, gazed out for a while then he looked back to the room and sat down on the chair next to his bed and the speech continued.

Should I ask dad to cancel it? . . . em. but no, I can't do that no! The family have probably concluded their arrangements! What should I do? damn it! He stuttered

Just then there came a knock on his door and his mother came in.

Mrs. Collins looked at Raphael, she observed how discomforted he had been.

Raphael are you ok? She asked him in a calm manner

Yes mom, I'm ok he tried to hide his discountenance.

She knew quite well that he's troubled.

Son. as she approached him.

You can always tell me anything at anytime no matter what it is.

Raphael looked at her and said

Mom, this is my gift and my ruin right?

She looked at him as if to say "what task?" but he went on)

It is my gift to heal people and make their pain go away . . . she nodded

Why can I not heal myself? And why do I feel helpless all the time? When I was a kid, I suffered amongst other kids and yet if they get sick, I'll be there to help them. This somehow mom, don't feel right, I don't want to be like this anymore mom, I'm so tired of being different." tears rolled down his eyes.

I'm tired mom, please help me!

With tears in her eyes. Went close to him, knelt down and said.

I will do anything to help you my son, anything . . . You're special and by you so many people have been blessed including me, yet you suffer and nobody can help you, it's unfair son, life is unfair . . .

She wiped her tears and wiped his and said with a strong voice

Raphael . . . I know that you are strong in your heart . . . . she paused and wiped her tears, then continued . . . Raphael, he looked up

"This is who you are. Be strong for me, for your family but above all for yourself . . . don't you give up!!!

Never give up! She told him

Raphael summoned courage and nodded a yes to her and wiped her tears off her eyes. she continued

You are going to give that girl back her life and the Lord will take care of you my son. Mrs Collins lamented.

Don't cry mom, you're right! The Lord will take care of me, I know that and I love you very much mom!

She hugged him and whispered into his ears.Be strong now my son, I love you Raphael!

Chief Okon had been looking for this day, the day her only daughter would recover and hopefully walk again. He had felt in-measurable guilt for that careless phone call that faithful day, that morning that has caused her young girl many years on a handicap chair. If only he could turn back the hands of time, he would not have made that call. He had been to many hospitals home and abroad but she could not be revalidated. He had been told by one of the doctors that Arei would in time regain the strength of the torn cross band ligaments in her both knees since she was just a child when the accident occurred and would eventually walk again. It gave him the hope that he had searched for and that she would walk again but that was over twenty years ago.

Mrs Okon was unlike him, she was not ardent about the whole set up, she did not believe that after all the known surgeons and revalidations, an unknown boy who had no medical experience would do them any good. She worried also of her status how her friends from the club would react to this when the news got out. She was a member of the millionaires club. The men played leisure time tennis while they share their interest in different deal proposals. The women grouped together and gossip away the moment as they sip on different kinds of liquor. Who bought what and who did not . . . new clothe designs and material things. They made sure that they had every other week a new cloth, shoes, diamond . . . it could be anything as long as it had not been worn before. She loved the attention. Mrs. Okon casually got ready with their escorts to bring down Arie, their sick daughter to the residence of Mr. and Mrs. Collins. She came down to the living room where Chief had long been waiting.

Darling, I still think that this is absurd . . . she said

Well, what would you suggest? He replied

She paused for a while and said . . . Instead we could look for more professional doctors, but considering some unknown African voodoo healing . . . but Chief would not let her finish, he said We've gone to over fifty doctors in different states and countries, none of them could even identify what she's suffering from. Torn ligaments has kept Arei from walking over decades. We have no more option and it could also not be worst that it already is, Agnes. He concluded. Whenever they would talk about her accident, it made him feel like a bad father, one who took from her the one thing he could not give back.

She went on, something about Dr. Jaffa he cuts in . . . Yeah! I know what doctor Jaffa said, listen darling, I'll do anything and pay any price to get our daughter healed but I've failed so far. This is her choice and we must grant it.

She is a sick girl looking for remedy. She will try anything because she's desperate, but we have to look out for her . . . she said

They had been engaged in that serious debate of 'if she should go' and would not notice that Arei had been behind them and had listened through all their conversation. When she had considerably engulfed enough she made them become aware of her presence and suddenly there was silence and her parents stood still, they gazed at her with lowered jaws which seemed to be full of unsaid words.

Oh honey, how long have you been listening. We were just making sure that it is the right place. She tried to crawl out of that fishy corner she had been put when she saw her.

What harm could it cost me . . . she asked with tears, So yes mother, I have listened long enough to hear your speech of what would be the best . . .

Oh baby, I am a worried parent and I am watching out for you. her mother said.

Yes darling, everything will be ok . . . We were trying to work this out for you. her father added.

Yes dad, I know, thanks! As for you mother, you only care about your so called high society image, what they are going to say when they hear that your sick daughter has left the highly paid surgeons to go after a sick boy with strange ability, isn't it mom? She fired at her. She hit her directly causing her to fiddle her fingers in panic. As a little girl, Arei had understood how being among the members of the high society had been her mother's priority. Her mother had been born into a family who would sell their soul to the devil and would ask for a the devil's receipt if it would get them anywhere near the known and famous people. Arei's grandmother would visit them dressed up in a manner that showed how sophisticated and high their society ranked. She always spoke to Arei of how a woman is supposed to be dressed with a proud posei. She often wondered how dad met her mother considering their difference in attitude.

No darling, I'll give anything at all to make you better. Arei's mother said

Her father supported and said . . . . My daughter, your mom is just looking out for you.

Dad, if she's really looking out for me let her respect my wish or at least pretend she does . . . I'll be in my room till you're ready to go.

She swung her wheel chair around and rolled away.

While Arie was rolling out of the scene, chief Okon's phone rang.

Chief Okon reluctantly took his phone, he had been devastated by that awkward conversation with Mrs Okon . . . Hello! He said to the person on the line.

Hello Chief, how are you? Said Mr. Collins

He immediately re-focused his attention to his main goal and said. Thank you Mr. Collins,

I'm fine.

We're set, my son is really in a good shape now. When will you arrive? He asked

Chief Okon said . . . I'll be right on my way, in another hour I should be there.

Mr. Collins continued . . . Very good . . . good, eh Chief Okon please, I would like you to bring the rest of my . . .

Chief cuts in and said to him . . . Very well Mr. Collins, goodbye. and hung up. He was irritated by his unhealthy love for money. He Called out to the house helps to prepare for the trip.

Raphael sat in his room with Nikki and Michael. He laid on his bed and read while Nikki and Michael struggled with a game on his desk.

His two siblings reminded him of the characters in the a cartoon movie. The cat and the mice. Each time they started something, it would end up in a struggle. Right there in his room, they were into one of those moments. The noise got louder by the minutes, he looked up to them and said . . . . Hey guys, knock it off, I'm trying to read.

Nikki the mouse said . . . oh It's Michael, he's always cheating.

Michael the cat replied . . . . No I'm not cheating, I'm just kicking your ass!

You call that ass kicking? She said

Oh yeah! He continued . . . They paid no attention but continued their stride for supremacy. He had been many times in the middle of their stride and he knew quite well how to handle them after all they are just his siblings.

Guys! Hey! Hey! He screamed, and they froze. Action and re-action are equal and opposite he muttered . . . Thank you! I want some attention from you guys. Sometimes you have to listen to me.

They stopped playing and turned to him. They appologized

Michael went first. Sorry man, really!

Nikki then Hopped on his bed and said . . . Are you alright?

Raphael said . . . Yeah., I just wanted you guys to slow down so I can do some reading. she hugged him, I know what will cheer you up. he said

What. he curiously asked. Nikki had many funny suggestions. She once suggested that Raphael should open up a clinic and perform his healings their as a surgeon. He had feared one of those kind of suggestions again.

A glass of chilled apple juice . . . she said. She knew how much he liked a cold glass of apple juice. Raphael would never say no to one. She could see the trace of thin smile run down his cheek as he said . . . Yeah, I would love to have one, but please, no more noise ok!

Cool! Michael said as he went back to the desk and Nikki stepped towards the door to get some apple juice.

Nikki, can you pour me a glass? Michael asked

Nikki hesitated to give an answer but she caught a glimpse of Raphael's face and said . . . Yeah, sure, coming right up sir. she opened the door and soured downstairs.

Michael and Raphael had just had a few minutes of silence when Nikki emerged. That was fast, Michael said as he turned to grab his glass of apple juice but Nikki had none and they look on her face was different. We have visit, she announced as the party ended.

The arrival of Chief, Agnes and Arei was welcomed by the Collins family. Their entourage crowded the living room with bags of gifts for the Collins family. It was an idea that Raphael never welcomed. For his troubles he demanded nothing. The happy faces of the use-to-be sick had been his satisfaction.

His mother was not very excited about it because it could cause him harm. The doctor's advice repeatedly rang in her head.

Mr. Collins Welcome Chief. we've been expecting you. This is my wife Angela. he said letting his finger point her out. Mrs Collins took a very small nod and smiled.

Thank you Mr. Collins . . . Madam, as Chief nodded back at Mrs Collins and went on to introduce his company. My wife Agnes, my lovely little girl Arei and these gentlemen who work for me. he finalized with a broadened cheek.

Hello Agnes. Arei and to you gentlemen, you are welcomed to my house. Mrs Collins started. You are most kind Madam. Arei said. She was not only graced facially but had a manner of speech that made her admirable amidst others. She got the awareness of Mrs Collins who in turn said . . . thank you lovely young woman.

Just then came in Raphael, Nikki and Michael.

Oh, please come kids, These are my children Nikki, Michael and Raphael. she said as she pointed them out.

Chief Okon who would not care too much about all the formalities, who would rather see her daughter instantly transformed to an able young woman than play this lets-get-to-know-eachother-game interrupted her . . . Beautiful young men and woman. And who is the wonder kid? He asked . . .

Mrs. Collins said . . . You must be referring to my son Raphael. she walked close to him. he neared them a bit but got the greatest surprise of his life . . . The girl on the wheel chair, the sick little Arei was the girl from his dream. He started sweating and felt dizzy. His head spinned around and almost made him hit the floor but he managed to excuse himself and ran back to his room.

She only existed in his dream. It looked to him like a he had fallen into another trance. If he had expected to ever meet her, this moment was far from it.

Mrs. Collins went after him the others stood in awe of this awkward first meeting. For the family Okon, they would have still been in shock and it would take some minutes of sanity to understand what just took place.

Adileo

Mr. Collins who thought about nothing but the rest of his wages took the centre stage and tried his shallow act of speech to entertain the visitors. Luckily the visitors still struggled in their minds to dilute the re-action of the one who they had hoped on. It was just like the aftermath of a high magnitude earthquake.

Mrs. Collins went after him in haste . . . Are you ok son? I can send them away.

Raphael replied . . . No mum, I'll be fine.

Son, you don't have to do this, you have done quite enough . . . she told him

Raphael answered . . . No mum, it's ok! Just let me be alone for a moment.

She kissed him and left

Raphael pep-talked himself . . . I can do this, she's the girl from my dreams, I must do this.

It is actually making sense. She was meant to be here. I am meant to help her. I've done this before and though she's the only person I'd seen in my dream prior to a healing, this is it, this must be something he concluded as he returned to the livingroom.

Mrs Okon said to him. Is everything ok with Raphael? She asked because she had never been in support of this venture.

Yes ma'am . . . I am fine, I apologize for my actions earlier. Raphael told them.

"Arei is everything I've got, I'll give you anything if you could make her walk again"

Chief supported her notion. They were ready for whatever price it would take to make her walk again. That was indeed no fallacy.

Raphael hardly paid attention to what they had been saying. He had his eyes fixed on her. She was so beautiful just like in his dreams. It felt like a déjà vu. Raphael had never been in love so he did not understand what he had felt.

In a moment he was lost into her, not realising how deep he had guessed at her, everyone in the room was amazed at that. Raphael's family never knew Raphael had a side that cared for woman. Raphael till now had been a virgin.

When he snapped out of his short trance with Arei, he said that he's ready for the "action". So he came close to her. he shook and fidgeted. He placed his palms on her's and trembled as he held fast. He looked deep into her eyes and she kept smiling. Most of the sick people he had cured would become afraid of him when he stared hard and close at them but she was so confident in him, he saw that through her angelic smile.

He could not explain what it was that made him helpless when he looked at her. Was it the smile or her face . . . Most of the others looked pale and weak.

He tried to concentrate and reach the inside of his strength, but he could not. With others it lasted couple of minutes but with her it had become different. He had never been afraid of healing, he never had to because his powers made their way through, he was just a vacuum, but with her he feared failure. He kept going and going but nothing seemed to work. He tried for hours but still nothing happened. She still looked sick and felt sick too. He become desperate and each time he looked up at her, she would give him that same smile. After five hours, he got tired for he had powers leaving him without fulfilling the aim.

Arei intelligent and patient noticed his despair, her family were disappointed, but she had not given up. Finally she said:

Daddy, we need to be alone, let everyone in the room leave us alone.

Amazingly she started giving the orders. She came to be healed and all of a sudden, she became the "she who had to be obeyed".

Chief Okon stood still, he starred at every face in confusion, unable to say a word. Mr. Collins the family Judas could not stand still. He paced up and down the room murmuring. He was about to be exposed of his ballad of inhuman dealings and probably get whooped by Chief's thugs.

Raphael's mother could not take the quietness any further so she broke the silence . . .

Son, maybe they should come another time.

Arei gentle said to her . . . Please Mrs. Collins, she was physically tired but mentally she could go on forever. She coughed and continued . . .

Please Madam, I beg you to let Raphael try once more. He can do it. Please she begged as she coughed even more.

Mrs. Collins said . . . . I don't think it's a good idea.

But Raphael just then turned to his mother and nodded a sign of "ok"

Oh! Raphael . . . she giggled, folded her hands over her breast and left and the others followed.

Alone in the room Raphael could barely look at Arei

Now we are alone, put yourself together and do what you've always done, heal me! Raphael . . . she sounded like his counselor.

Ok! I will try . . . he said as if he had been re-enforced by her pep.

Arei said . . . . Remember! You can do it, if you can't it's ok but you have to try again. Only you can heal me . . . She encouraged him with that same vigorous smile. He would be the one that would differenciate her from ever walking again or being on that damned wheel chair for the rest of her life. He was her last hope.

Without saying a word he understood all that. He had the intention of healing her but his powers doesn't work in accordance to his intentions and he knew that. He stared at her, but this time he took a heavy deep breath, took her hands and closed his eyes. He held her hands firmly and in a second he started trembling and a huge amount of power came off him. Like lightening and went from his head down through his hands into her. In a moment they were both wrapped in a cloud of smoke like a great furnace was heating . . . When the smoke cleared, behold there she stood on her feet, transformed into an astonishing young, hubsch and pretty damsel.

Her sickness had left her, the use of her legs totally restored. She wasn't lame anymore, she had been wholesomely made well.

He laid there on the floor motionless in a sea of his own sweat.

He woke up at the hospital with a blur view which was just enough to see the feminine image that sat by the side of his bed.

He opened his eyes, tried to keep them open while he gazed at her.

At first he thought it was Nikki but the more he could vividly view that female, the more clear it became to him that Nikki would be more smaller than her.

He's awake! She screamed out to the others with a smile. The others came running into the room. She was the girl he had cured. it was Arei.

Mrs. Collins called out to him . . . Raphael! Raphael! Can you hear me son?

He turned his head and nodded slightly.When he saw it was her sitting by his bed, he was glad and with a smile he expressed his delight to see her.

Mrs. Collins continued . . . Oh, thank God! You scared us son. We've been worried about you. she looked up and thanked the Almighty for not allowing such tragedy.

Oh! Thank you God!

My son is alive, he's ok! Oh! Thank you Papa God!

Raphael replied in a tiny shaky voice, Raphael turned to his mother and said.

How long have I been here . . . he asked her

She looked at him and paused, then look at the others in the room, piteously she said. Raphael my son, you have been here for a week now, even the doctor told us it's uncertain what might happen.

Raphael raised his tired eyeballs and said . . .

Oh, God . . . for a week!! I'm sorry mum.The sense of being a burden to his mother made him feel terrible. He felt very bad.

He tried sitting up but his head hurt so much that he felt like an un-going construction project was taking place in his head so he quickly laid back.

Michael said to him . . . Raphael, please relax. The doctor said that you'll need a lot of rest if you plan to gain consciousness any time soon, you know.

Nikki almost immediately added . . . We thought for a while that we lost you Raphael, but I told them that you'll make it, I knew it. She smiled trying to hide her devastating worries.

Mr Collins did not bother, he had finally nailed it. the deal had been sealed and his money would be cashed . . . Poor Raphael, he had again been used and left out there to die.

Mrs. Collins went on . . . Thank God that you are alive, don't worry about anything. I will be here with you, I'm not going nowhere son, you hear that! Yes your mother is here.

He nodded gently and smiled. He turned around and looked at the girl by his bedside, a new face but familiar, could this be it. he thought. She looked even more pretty than he remembered in his trance.

May life give me another chance to know her better, she may be the nucleus of my life. Raphael silently prayed.

Arie kept smiling, kindly and passionately.Suddenly, wooziness hit him and he felt like she was fading away, he tried to keep her from going, he struggled to keep his eyes open but the medications he had been infused made sure he rested. She smiled on till her face disappeared just as he fell back into slumber.

Chief Okon celebrated his life away. He was happy exceedingly. He had not seen Arei a lot at home since she got well but he did not mind. He walked to his bar/fridge and poured himself a glass of scotch with some ice cubes in it. He took the glass danced and pace up and down his living. Mrs. Okon joined him shortly.

Are you ok . . . She said to him he kept dancing and and sipping his alcohol without a word so she repeated her question again, this time making sure she was audible enough.

My dear, is everything alright . . . She said again

Chief Okon finally looked at her with a relief and satisfaction and simultaneously he said

Is everything alright . . . Of course! This is the happiest moments of my life! He smiled and sipped.

My daughter is a healthy girl and happy. No amount of money could bring me such happiness.

Yes my dear, that is true. That boy is a great gift from above, but my dear how do we tell people this story? How do we explain to friends when they ask about it? She worried

It wont be difficult, the story can not be hidden, the boy's power should not be hidden. We would tell anyone who asked exactly what happened. He answered as he took even a longer sip out of his glass.

Mrs. Okon continued . . . But my dear, it's a bit complicated! Our friends in the club might think that we couldn't afford the medical expenses, so we resolved to some spiritual aid. You are a rich man with connections in high places, don't you think we might have to be careful what we say. she said.

I'll tell you what I think!! I think that I've been rich while my daughter had been sitting on a wheel chair, handicapped, deprived of so many things physically and emotionally! My riches could not help her. So I don't care what my so called friends may think. My daughter can walk now my dear, and that for me is a million times more worthy than the club, friends and riches my dear. You know what they say, friends, money and things will come and go but family remains for all time . . . he sipped up his drink and poured himself a fresh glass of another brand and staggered to the sofa with a half full glass of a brownish fluid. She stood there and watched him with her hands folded over her bossom.

The greedy man who had turned Raphael's phenomenal powers into an investment had only been concerned for Raphael because of his financial gains.

He laid down on his bed contemplating on how to carry on more mischievous plans without his treachery uncovered.

I hope Raphael stays alive, that boy has made me a fortune and I need more . . . he would always tell himself with an evil smile.

He got up and sat by the edge of the bed and continued to talk to himself.

I still have some unfinished business with Chief . . . he muttered

He went to pick his phone and suddenly it rang, he gazed at the number on his screen and immediately he noticed who the caller was., he cleared his throat and answered . . .

Hello!. He said in a faked depressed voice.

Mrs. Collins was on the line. Hello, hello! She shouted

He replied . . . Yes I'm here, how is Raphael my son? I'm missing him! Tell me please!. he lied . . . .

Don't you worry my husband, your son is back and alive! He had just spoken to us a few minutes ago . . . she happily told him.

Mr. Collins said. Oh yes! I mean thank you Lord! Please let me talk to him, I want to make sure it's true! I want to hear him!. He had hoped it was true and that meant that he would be back in business.

Mrs. Collins replied . . . It is true, our son is ok but he's sleeping now. As soon as he gets up we'll call you.

Ok! But make sure he calls me as soon as he wakes up ok! Don't forget! Bye! He puts down the phone and celebrated for the restoration of his cruel deals.

Yes! I'm back in business! Make money! Make money money money! He sang as he danced to his melody. I have to make a call right away. He took his phone and dialled just as he pulled a stick of cigar, light it up and inhaled it several times. He stood still as the smoke rushed out of his nose and mouth simultaneously, he puffed the smoke into the air.

Raphael gently opened his eyes this time without difficulties. He had started to regain his strength and consciousness. Nobody was in the room except Arei. He smiled at her with snoozzy eyes and Arei said.

Hey voyager! Welcome home, you've been sleeping peacefully. The doctor said it was good for your recovery. It's good to have you back . . . She smiled Thank you he answered. he was shy, he couldn't look at her face squarely. Where's my mother. he asked as if it was all that he could think of, though having his mother in the room at that moment was the last thing on his mind.

Arei said. Your mother . . . Oh yeah . . . em, she just left to make a call, to your father I guess.

She is an impressive woman . . . she hailed her, he nodded and she went on . . .

Let me see if she's done, i will get her right away. She tried to get up

But Raphael had motioned with his hands for her to hold . . .

Oh no, no, don't worry. Don't interrupt her. When mother goes on the phone she stays a while . . . he added and they looked at each other and both smiled.

Arei said . . . Well . . . That's typical for mothers

But Raphael in a tired cracked voice said

You mean women . . . he smiled

They both laughed, she has still the same charming beam he had always remembered in his dreams and he said

What's your name and who are you . . .

Arei looked down to her feet as if she was trying to avoid that question and she said . . . We've done this before, have you forgotten. You know my name and who I am.

She smiled.

I'm sorry but I'm a bit shaken and I did forget some things that I used to know. Only I still remember where I saw you for the first time. He said as he stared at her.

Arei said. you mean at your house, while I was on my wheel chair . . .

No, in my dream. You are the girl from my dream. Your face is the same, your smile I'll never forget.

And she smiled at him but he continued. She thought, it was a very floppy line to use but it did not matter to her.

These dreams didn't happen once but kept repeating over and over again. he said. Now she had started to like the use-to-be—floppy line. he went on

Arei With a smile on her face she said to him, that was good, I just hope. He moped at her without really following what she meant . . . she continued

I hope your girlfriend doesn't hear this.

Raphael smiled but carefully, smiling all the way would cause him more headaches.

No she wont! I promise you . . . he said jokingly

Ok, that's good to hear for our own safety . . . she added

She won't hear this because I have no girlfriend. I've never had one. I'm 20 years old and still don't have any. he smiled awkwardly.

Arie passionately said . . . I'm really sorry to raise that topic . . . She was relieved that he was still free, that meant no competitors but she concealed it like such thought would never cross her mind.

Raphael interrupted her . . . Don't apologise, it's not necessary. People don't miss what they don't know or have. Besides, who wants a freak for a boyfriend. He said as he looked at her.

She could see how disappointed he sounded and it touched her heart.

She lived just in the same world as his. She said to him

You may be a freak, but you are a special freak . . . a freak who made me well. She smiled with emotions.

"You are not a freak but a very special person with a healing gift. You are far from a freak and someday some girl will recognise that and make you happy."

Just then the doctor walked into the room with Raphael's family who followed to hear his analysis. The doctor had run many test to understand what is going with Raphael. Why he would pass out in many occasions. It was the same doctor he had had since his childhood. Dr.

Van Alst had devoted a lot of time following this mystery of Raphael. For many years, he could not come up with a logical explanation to his powers but he believed that it did depreciate his physical well being. He had formed with co-doctors a league of specialist devoted to understanding how the boy had come to such powers. It finally came to their knowledge and he had told Raphael's mother that. He was curiously followed by Mrs Collins,

Nikki and Michael as he came into the hospital room.

Agnes did her morning duty which was about nothing. Every morning she got up to a well cleaned house, polished floors and sweetly prepared meal. She owe that to Chief's luxurious mode of living. House helps did just about every thing. But that morning, Agnes supervised every detail of the work being done. She had invited some of her club friends over to the house. They're two women: Catherine and Kate.

She had waited for that day, she enjoyed the company of her co-gossips. The house was empty, Chief had gone out for business and Arei had been spending a lot of time at the hospital where Raphael had been admitted.

47

The doorbell clings, she quickly answered, Catherine and Martha stood at the door. They were dressed well.

Catherine seemed alot older than Martha but her style made her fit into whatever age she was willing to admit. She had a tight silky brown dress and a brown coat. She was a plus sized woman. You could see her extra curves poking out from her side. She was a tall and a huge lady. She had a very pronounced make up, one you could see from a mile away. She had a sweet fragranced perfume.

Her counter part was new in the millionaires club. They just moved into town. She dressed herself in a simple grey linen trousers, an orange top and a scarf in orange to match her top, some flat dark shoes and a grey hand bag. She had a very beautiful sun shade on.

Hello Agnes . . . Catherine said

As she walked in and Martha followed behind . . .

She took off her coat while she introduces Martha

You know Martha from the club, the wife of our pilot . . . . Catherine continue.

Oh, yeah, how can I forget. Agnes answered rather un-thrilled. she smiled at Martha and went ahead of Catherine as she whispered to her.

What's the meaning of this, I thought you and Kate are coming over.

And quickly she turned to Martha with a fake smile.

Kate had other plans, I suggest we party without her, she wouldn't mind! Catherine answered sarcastically to Agnes and then turned to Martha with a fake smile as well then she said,

Martha, darling, this is Agnes. She's a very lovely lady.

Catherine turned and stared at Agnes as if to say 'be nice to her' in a wordless manner.

Hello Agnes, I've heard a lot about you . . . said Martha

Oh, don't listen to those talks. Can I hang your jacket up for you . . . Agnes offered

Sure! Thank you. She said . . . She was pretty, a lady with a small stature. She was in her middle thirties. She was the youngest female in the millionaires club which had automatically earned her the hottest and for the older women the most hated member of the rich gossip group.

Make yourself at home and I'll be right back with some drinks. What would you like to drink . . . she asked

Martha replied . . . . A glass of white wine will do, thanks.

Coming up Agnes said as she turned to Catherine and said . . . I can use a help in there . . . she pointed to the kitchen.

Of course . . . Catherine answered almost immediately and went to the kitchen with her.

I told you to stop showing up with strangers in my house. I don't know any pilot's wife in the club. This is just your way of avoiding Kate because of your last fight, isn't it . . . Agnes accused Catherine.

She knew her too well.

So! . . . Maybe it is but Martha is nicer than Kate.

Why do you even bother yourself about that arrogant madam . . . Catherine said

How do you know that she is better than Kate, she's just been here for a very short time besides we have been having this gathering for a long time with Kate . . . Agnes replied

Are we going to argue about this and feel ridiculous all day or have some fun she asked her.

Ok! But for the record, you're being mean to Kate. Thought you should know it! Agnes concluded

Whatever! . . . . I need some of your strongest scotch, I'm in the mood for a party. Your daughter's story need to be told . . . Catherine said as they went back to meet Martha and started drinking and gossiping. After a long time of heavy drinking, they started to get drunk, especially Catherine.

The door bell rang and there stood Kate.

Agnes was shocked at the sight of Kate and what seemed to have been a party went sour.

Kate! What are you doing here? I thought you have other plans . . . was the reaction of Agnes

Kate Didn't answer, she walked in to the direction of the ladies with an intention.

Now you know how to party without me. she asked. You're drinking scotch and malts without inviting me. her questions continued. So that's how it is now? Agnes! I came to congratulate you for your daughter's health but I can see that you're having already enough congratulations from that one . . . as she points to Catherine.

I introduced Catherine to you and all of a sudden she had become more important to you than i am.

No Kate. It's not like that! Agnes said knowing very well that the party was about to go ablaze.

Yes it's like that, so what? Catherine bragged

Please Catherine, don't start! Said Agnes

Catherine who had drinking for a while, intoxicated by alcohol could not hold her peace.

Don't start!. she asked as she tried to stagger to her feet . . . You let her walk in here and talk to us like that and you do nothing . . .

Martha sat there speechless. She almost drowned in her own stillness. She was just caught up

In a mix, she managed to say . . . Hello Kate, my name is Martha . . . but she scowled at her and she quietly retired to her sit. I guess a scowl was all she needed.

Catherine continued to express her discountenance of Agnes. How could you tolerate someone to walk in to your house and verbally abuse your visitors with no regards for you.

I thought we are friends from the same club. Lets be matured and reasonable please! Agnes said.

Kate answered her . . . Yeah, that's what I thought till now . . . Nothing about her is reasonable . . . she pointed at Catherine.

Catherine raged at her . . . That's it! You know what . . . You are lucky that it's not in my house.

I would have turned you upside down. She meant with the use of violence.

Martha! Come lets go! She shouted. Martha sprung to her feet like a soldier and made towards the door, it had been an unforgettable meeting for her.

Agnes pursued them pleading . . . No please! Wait Catherine! Martha. lets settle this as adults ladies, common now lets take a deep breath have a drink and think things over. she kept preaching but those words fell on deaf ears as the women rattled against each other.

Catherine who already stood up, grabbed her coat and made for the door. Cursing as she went and Martha at her trail, at the door she stopped and looked at Agnes and said . . .

I can't believe that this could happen in your house and you call yourself a member of the million dollars club, this is almost as ridiculous as the stupid story of how your daughter got healed. If you had no money for a proper hospital, then ask for help. She stood for some seconds as she sized Agnes up with her callous stare and in drunken steps went out of the door, Martha followed behind, she made a sorry face and banged the door behind her.

I saw that one coming Agnes . . . said Kate as she chuckled turned and said to her

Is it worth it? Welcome to the million dollars club . . . Kate opened the door and left while

Agnes stood in the middle of the room frozen and thwarted.

The boy had been reported to be ok. His plans. his evil plans sprung back to life.

Mr Collins was born in Lagos. A city of over fifteen million people in the south of Nigeria. A

Yaruda by tribe. Partying and money profligacy was the other of the day of his ethnic diversity.He loved the idea of being rich more than how rich he could ever be. So he became ignorant of his egoistic personality.

Mr Collins who had stayed the whole while plotting how to expand his trade, the trade of

'benevolence exploitation' decided it was time to seek further disfigured, blemished and ill people whom he would send to Raphael. He figured that the more he gathered the better it becomes for his pocket.

He knew he had to act quick because he could soon be caught. But before that it was time to set the book straight with Chief so he picked up his phone and dialled Chief Okon. Hello chief, how are you today . . . said Collins

Chief Okon had expected that call . . . Hello Mr Collins, I'm feeling good, thank you and how's everything going. replied Chief. Oh Very well, thank you chief . . . answered Collins. Chief could feel his anxiety but he went ahead and asked him . . . Any news about your son from the hospital. Yes, just had my wife on the phone and there's good news, he would be out soon.

He had not neared the hospital nor seen Raphael till that moment. He talked sweetly about how he had been at the hospital and how much his son suffered. He had hoped that Chief Okon would give him more money than he would initially acquire.

Chief Okon was a kind man. He was very happy to hear that the boy had recovered from his coma but he was more delighted that his daughter was no longer disabled.

Very good indeed, I'm glad, that son of your's have changed my view of things as regards to life, now I see life differently and it's amazing how little things can be of great significance.
Chief said.

Mr. Collins thanked him hurriedly, he cleared his throat in preparation of his speech, then he said, but Chief I called to know how we should settle the rest of our . . . Chief Okon knew quite well where he was driving at, he broke through his unfinished speech and said to him

Your money! Just come over when you can and get the remaining of your money, I have it prepared anytime.

Mr Collins was thrilled to hear that. Again he drew his breath and said, I don't want to seem too hasty but can i come now if it's ok . . .

Sure! I'm sorry I've been busy lately. an agreement is an agreement, your money is ready. Chief said civilly.

Precisely my point Collins said as he let run down his chin a cruel giggle . . . Since you have it now I'll be on my way, Raphael's hospital costs needs to be paid today.

Ok, Mr Collins . . . anwsered Chief Okon.

Mr Collins hung up the phone and quickly got dressed, he toddled back to the living room and sipped the rest of his whisky, he gazed around to make sure nothing had been left behind then zoomed to the door and vanished.

The doctor walked into Raphael's room while he talked with Arei. The both looked at him and seized their blether for later.

Dr Van Alst was an elderly fellow with a pointed jaw. He had a dark curly hair with patches of grey hair scattered all over his head. His pointed jaw was neatly shaved. He was tall and slender and he wore always a small smile.

Good-day Raphael, how are you. Dr Alst asked. For a doctor who smiled often he looked solemn and there was something about his attitude that made Raphael uncomfortable. He did not seem to be happy, he looked frazzled and nervous.

Hello doctor, I'm getting better. Raphael smiled as he looked over his shuolder at Arei who nodded yes towards the doctor.

Can I have a word with Raphael alone . . . the doctor requested

Yes please, they answered as they all made for the door. Mrs Collins asked the doctor if it was necessary to leave him by himself . . . Let me stay please, she asked but the doctor insisted so she joined the rest at the hall way.

She turned to Raphael and said I'll be down the hall way.

Arei hurried back and gave Raphael a kiss, his ever first kiss, she smiled held his palm, Arei was just about leaving when Raphael said . . .

Its ok doc, you may tell me I want her to be here.he smiled back at her.

Are you sure about that . . . Dr Alst asked

Raphael said . . . yes, i am.

Arei repeated the words of the doctor but held him firmly as she smiled affectionately to him,

Raphael waggled without saying a word.

Doctor Van Alst understood that those two had fallen in love and it made his discovery even more had to say. He coughed lightly and started his narration . . . I'm afraid that the last scan of your brain showed an acute brain tumur. Arie was shocked as she turned and looked at him and the doctor paused for a while as if he meant to give him time to digest what he just heard, then he coughed again and went on. the tumur has eaten deep to your obulangata which controls the total human function. the doctor tried to keep his voice from trembling as he finally said, the increase in size is huge, it is now ninetyfive percent uncurable . . . I'm sorry . . . .

Raphael gazed at him all the while. He said nothing.

He had dreamt of many wild circumstances, he had even dreamt many times about death but he never thought he would be that close.

He knew that something wasn't coherent with him but nobody could tell him what it was.

As a child, he got sick often but had never been restored to health by pills. He healed with time.

His family heard the cry of Arei as she blasted out in tears, they came in and heard of

Raphael's critical situation, the hospital room turned into a turmoil.

Raphael asked the doctor what it meant in plain words and he answered . . . You will die . . . I'm not sure when but maximum two weeks . . . I'm sorry kid.

This was one of the moments Dr Van Alst had wished not to be a physician.

No! you must be mistaken . . . he's beginning to feel better . . . there's gotta be a better explaination Arei bewailed. She had falling in love to the one that gave her back her wellbeing.

Raphael, a strong looking and charming young man. She had spend many days at the hospital with him, she found him, the exceptional one. but now she's loosing him before she could even get to know him. Her joy has turned into grief. Was it her fault . . . would she be held liable to his recent dilemma . . . could the last curing be conscientious to Raphael's situation. could she have brought bereavement to the one that cured her. the one she had falling in love with . . . All this questions triggered her mind as she cried her eyes out.

Raphael's family had been struck with the most atrocious news, the room was crammed with weeping.

I wish i am wrong . . . I really do wish I am, said Dr Alst as he exited the room. A man commonly known as one of the hospitals premium surgeon.

Raphael was stock-still, he didn't know what to say or do. He knew that his life was not like most of the people he had known, he was from another sphere. He gazed as they all cried but he did not give up a tear.

The lamentation had died down and everyone sobbed and moaned in weariness.

Raphael sat up and said . . . Mother, please take Michael and Nikki home, you've been here all the day long, it will not change my fate. Go and eat something, take a shower, takecare of yourselves . . .

No, I can't leave you here. his mother replied in sniffle. She thought about the promise she had made over twenty years ago to a dying woman. How she had vowed to take care of him. She felt helpless and it weakened her. Raphael had been the foundation of her whole world. The child who had mystically unlocked her womb. He had given her the satisfaction of every woman. Watching him die would vary her wonderfully made life. She was not about to leave that room because as long as she stayed, Raphael must not die, so she thought . . . I will not run off on you my son, she insisted.

Please don't mourn me while I'm still alive, everybody should go home and have some rest. I need sometime to myself . . . Raphael demanded.

Please Raphael, let us stay here with you. Arei pleaded

Michael and Nikki joined up . . . Yeah Raph! Don't send us away . . . you could be in need of our help. the pleaded

Mrs Collins was about to continue when Raphael cut in . . .

Sorry mom, I feel very bad when I see all of you like this, I need sometime. Please, go now and come back tomorrow all of you as he turned and faced the window by his bedside.

Mrs Collins saw that he is in profound agony, she said;

Ok you've heard him. Respect your brother's wish now we'll come back in the

Morning. Her voice trembled as she said those words.

Michael interrupted her . . . but mama, that is unwise. We can't leave him . . . . He was still saying those words when Mrs Collins said to him. I want to stay too Michael but I'll listen to your brother and so should You . . .

Mrs Collins touched Raphael on his shoulder, he turned his face from the window back to them and they all gave him a hug.

Arie had no more tears left to shade so she only sobbed . . . You are always in my heart, she said to him as she sobbed through the door and out of the room.

Raphael watched them leave and tears dropped down his jowl.

Arei got home, she let herself in quietly trying to avoid everyone. She saw a man that looked like Raphael's father talking with her father. first she intended going in to make acquaintance but she stopped when she heard the two talk about Raphael and the money. Inquisitively, she got closer quietly and listened.

Chief I thank you for having the money in place, I can now settle Raphael's bills, the glutton started.

It is not a problem! We had an agreement, my daughter is well and you get your money, Chief replied with a tumbler of alcohol in his hand. He had offered one to Mr Collins but he had other things in mind so he declined.

I also appreciate your co-operation in keeping it off the record, its very necessary that my family know nothing about this matter, Mr Collins persisted.

Chief Okon nodded a yes without saying a word, he sipped from his glass and rolled his tongue over the drink in a discerning manner and said, I've been meaning to ask you this, though it's your business but all the same I'm curious, Why do you keep it undisclosed, he asked;

Mr Collins came closer to him as if he was about to let him in on a secret, he robbed his chin with his right hand, then he took a deep gulp of air and said, the lesser you know the healthier it is . . . . and Chief, no offence, he added haughtily.

Chief Okon was flabbergasted at his response. He deliberated that something was not right but it was not his problem so he said, no offence taken Mr Collins. Like I said, my daughter is well and the rest is trivial . . . the cash is all yours, as he handed him a puffed-up bundle of cash in an envelop.

I would love to stay and have a chat but I have bills to pay, you are a good man chief, he said as he quickly grabbed the cash and head for the door.

So long Mr Collins . . . . the door slammed behind Mr Collins.

What a bizarre man. Chief said as he sipped the remains of the scotch in his tumbler.

Arie had listened through all their tête-à-tête. She was puzzled but she doesn't have to be a whiz kid to understand what just happened.

She felt so awful for Raphael. She realised that Raphael had been a vacuum for Mr Collins affluence. Poor soul, been used and left to die. Great guilt came over her, she decided to go back to the hospital and see how he's doing, though she doesn't know how he'll react when he would see her. For the moment, Arei needed time to digest what she just saw, telling Raphael would absolutely be hazardous.

At the hospital, Raphael was still struggling to understand the fact that he'll be dead in seven days, at most in fourteen days. He was distressed with himself, with life, with his ill lot. He wondered how death would be like, if he would really meet people on the other side, missing his mum and affectionate family, the girl from his trance whom he had just healed and madly in love with. He couldn't handle it.

He regretted that he had sent them home. In a time like that, he needed someone to talk to, a shoulder to cry on, someone to soothe him, he had sent his mother, Arei the girl of his dream, his lovely brother and sister, he had in a moment of great soreness and perplexity send off his cherished ones.

He was in stillness all by himself in that deadly solitude. Death could not be as scary as the torment he was passing through. He was drowning in his own sweat and he could hear his heart pound a million times per second. He had in several times thought that he was already dead. If wishes were horses he would ride down to abyss himself, it would not be worse than how he had felt.

While he struggled on with his pre-dicament, he had a gentle knock on his door. He turned and watch the door open and what he saw was a female clothed in immaculate white mantle, she floated on a portion of a white cloud. She smiled at him and said Raphael my offspring, do not be troubled for we are family. Your place is here and it's prepared. Do not be troubled. Raphael looked close and rigid to her but the glow behind would not let him focus. He tried even harder but the woman was taken away and he saw her no more.

Raphael still baffled and bewildered, he took another look now the woman was gone and he saw that the door was still locked, it had not been opened like he thought. He thought he had seen a phantom, maybe one that was sent to get him. He was still recovering from this odd occurance when he heard another gentle knock. He expected another ghost but then Arei came in and directly she said:

Listen Raphael, I know you wanted to be alone which is your right, I shouldn't have dashed in here like this except for an urgent situation. The truth is that I can't live with myself if I don't tell you, it's driving me insane. She kept going on and on, then he said to her

Relax Arei., I'm relieved that you're here, I thought you were a ghost. He did not want to go further so he said . . . If there is one person I really want to see, it's you.

Really . . . I mean are you sure, because I can give you . . .

Raphael interrupted her and said . . . . Yeah, I'm sure, Just tell me what you want to say ok

And relax I'm happy to see you. He now knew how much he needed company. Arei was just a perfect shoulder for his distress.

Arie went close and held his hands with a grin. She looked up to him in tears and hugged him firmly as if he could evaporate without admonition. She was heart wrecked though he was there. How long was the subject she could not get out of her mind . . . how long will you live my dear Angel, she wondered.

She hesitated, she's not sure if it's right to tell him what she had just discovered about her father and Mr Collins. He's a dying chap who deserved to be pleased and enjoy his numbered days on earth. At the other hand she couldn't exonerate herself if he died without knowing what his father had done. She decided to feel his last times with glee, pleasure and love and leave the rest for the living. She gave him a kiss and caressed his upper body while he held her close.

I've never been this close to a female before, Raphael admitted

You're doing enormous Raphael, you're doing great my Angel, she told him.

She kissed him again and again. She went and locked the door and came to his bed.

Today you'll be a man in bliss and not a dying man, Arei said. This moment had waited for them for a long time and now even onto death, life was still worth living.

I have been waiting for it, now I know for what cause I was born, he said as they kissed and hissed.

He had been born for love and happiness and his kiss would remain on her lips long after he was gone.

Then take me Raphael and make love to me. Let me hold you in my arms, kiss you and make you my love, my first and right love. This would be the one night she would not disregard. Please make love to me, She cuddled Raphael and in all those agonizing days that moment he was not afraid of death.

They made love avidly and for two virgins, it was an etched on their minds experience.

One full of love and friendliness, untainted and pristine, a perfect romance. The whole night long they made each other comprehend the meaning of life.

Mr Collins drove away from Chief's house with pocket jam-packed with money, he smoked all the way as he raced than the road in total satisfaction. His handset rang, it was Mrs Collins.

She was about to tell him of the sad news. He had a stick of cigar in his mouth, he tried to pick his phone as it kept ringing next to him, a big hunk of the cigar ash dropped on his pants, they were hot and burned through his trousers.He tried to answer his phone and put the sizzling ash out at the same time and so he had no hands on the wheels. His car ran off the road and cracked into a tree, he had no seat belt on.

He was found hours later and he had been completely battered by the crash, broken ribs and jaws and he had entirely lost his memories and can no longer use his legs. After several Months of effortless rehabilitation and psychotherapy at the hospital where Raphael died, he was moved to a psychiatrc home where he lived as a handicapped cripple.

The iniquities of men lives after them, but the sins of Mr Collins had finally and brutally caught up with him, karma. He was divorced by Mrs Collins after Arie had told her what he did. He lived the rest of his life alone outside of the depressed without visits from his wife and children in a handicapped home and had lost all his memories. Money is not the root of all evil but irrepressible love for money is the root of all evil.

Raphael my angel as Arei fondly called him had been dead now for two years.

Arei often visit his grave with his mother, brother and sister to beautify them with flowers and sweet bouquet. She would sit and converse endlessly to the dead. She knelt down over the grave and reflected on the last days of his life, how they got closer and did things as one. How much love and delight he brought her way. How he had restored her feet back to her.

He had opened another door of life to her and she would forever be thankful to him. She wrote him a small letter, it read "Before I breathe my last . . . let me live, before I live . . . let me love, for lo! It is thy love that hast lent me wings with which i flew over troubled waters, hope had became a vibrant realism, now I am voyaging onto the sunrise and onto the dawning of a new beginning".

Raphael my love, it's gone on over three years since your gone but I still see you every day. I hold you every day. Your love remains with me forever. You changed my life in every way and I owe it to you!

She kissed her palm and placed it on the tomb.

She got up to leave and a kid came running up to her in those tiny adorable feet, the kid called out to her; Mama . . . Mama . . .

She picked him up and gave him a kiss. Say goodbye to your father she said as they both walked away into the beautiful sunset.

"WE ARE WHO WE ARE . . . WE MAKE POSITIVE CHANGES IN THE LIVES OF THOSE WE MEET WHEN WE LEARN TO ACCEPT WHO WE REALLY ARE"

THE END

The Meaning of LIFE is the title of my book.

Biography:

Leo Uzoma was born in Portharcourt the rainy city of Eastern Nigeria in 1978.

He was brought up in several cities of one of the great Ancient Songhai states.

He left the shores of Africa at sixteen to pursue his professional soccer carrer in

Europe.He was raised by a single mother after the ill-timed death of his father.

During his stay in Belgium, Germany, Austria and Netherlands he had gone through so many situations and too many experiences and all those amounted to his creativity and style with which he unfolded to us this piece of masterwork.

SUMMARY